# BIRDWATCHING

## Dr Terry Jennings

### Illustrated by Gary Rees

Hodder
Children's
Books

a division of Hodder Headline plc

Please note that the drawings of birds in this book are not to scale.

Text copyright 1998 © Dr Terry Jennings
Illustrations copyright 1998 © Gary Rees
Published by Hodder Children's Books 1998

Consultant: Sylvia Sullivan RSPB

Series design by Fiona Webb
Book design by Don Martin

The right of Terry Jennings and Gary Rees to be identified as the author
and illustrator of the work has been asserted by them in accordance with
the Copyright, Designs and Patents Act 1988.

10 9 8 7 6 5 4 3 2 1

A catalogue record for this book is available from the British Library.

ISBN: 0 340 71584 7

Printed by Clays Ltd, St Ives plc.

Hodder Children's Books
a division of Hodder Headline plc
338 Euston Road
London NW1 3BH

# Meet the author

Terry Jennings is a former teacher and university lecturer. He has been interested in birds, natural history and the countryside for as long as he can remember. He has written more than 150 books for children and teachers and has studied birds and other kinds of wildlife in many countries of the world. He now lives in a village in Norfolk, within easy reach of some of the best bird-watching areas in Britain. His wife and four children share his love of birds and the countryside.

# Introduction

Birds are brilliant! A blackbird singing, a bluetit doing acrobatics, seagulls soaring overhead, a tame robin feeding at the window, a huge flock of starlings wheeling across the sky... which will you see or hear today? These are just a few of the 550 species of birds which live in or visit the British Isles – all different, and all fascinating in their own way.

Birdwatching is a wonderful hobby. You can watch birds everywhere – in the middle of a city or on a remote island. This book tells you some of the ways you can learn more about wild birds without moving too far from home. (But do remember to tell your parents what you are doing, where you are going, and who you are going with.) There is still much that scientists do not know – even about common birds such as house sparrows and blackbirds. With this book, you can go beyond looking for 'new' birds, to the even more rewarding task of finding out about the habits and behaviour of birds. This is the way to become a real ornithologist!

The bad news about birds is that their habitats are rapidly disappearing. Even common birds like the song thrush, skylark and tree sparrow are becoming rarer. But don't despair! There are lots of people who care about birds and work hard to protect them, and you can be one of them. The more you find out about birds, the more you will be able to do to help them.

Good luck, and have fun!

Terry

# Contents

# What every birdwatcher needs

## Equipment

If you go to some quiet parts of the coast, you may well see a birdwatcher looking like this:

Birdwatchers love bits of kit and it's a wonder some of them don't do themselves an injury carrying it all. To be fair, all of this gear can be very useful at times, but it costs a lot of money and is not essential. Also, you might make so much noise staggering along with it that you scare all the birds away.

Birdwatching doesn't have to be an expensive hobby. To start with all you need are two sets of things you already have – your eyes and ears. You also need a notebook and pencil, and a good bird identification book.

For making notes out-of-doors, a stout notebook which fits easily in your pocket is best. Choose one with stiff covers, since this makes writing and sketching easier. A thick rubber band will keep the notebook closed and stop the pages becoming too dog-eared.

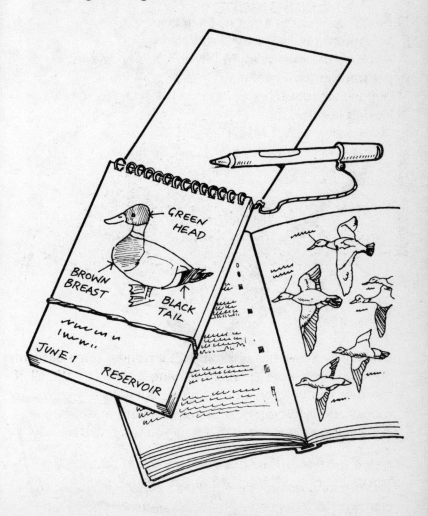

## RSPB* advice to young ornithologists

- Take care not to harm any living thing
- Protect your local, natural environment
- Try to be environmentally friendly both at home and at school
- Find out about the threats to the planet and try to help reduce them
- Have fun sharing what you know with others and help them to enjoy and care about wildlife and the environment

*Royal Society for the Protection of Birds

### Did you know?

*Around the world 1,100 bird species are in danger of extinction. They include 146 British birds.*

The other essential is a good guide book which shows the different bird species in colour. Coloured drawings are usually better than coloured photographs, because the birds can be shown from different angles. The best bird books point out special features in the bird's build or colouring which help to identify it.

But don't rush out and buy a bird book right away. Borrow a selection from the library and try them out on a bird you can see from a window at home. Pretend you have never seen that bird before and try to identify it using one of the books. Are the pictures in the book accurate? Does it show the robin's breast the right shade of red? Is the house sparrow the right shape? Does the starling look real? Only when you have tested several bird identification books in this way, should you think about buying one.

As most of us cannot write neatly when we are walking or standing about outdoors, you may want to have another, 'best' book in which to copy out your bird notes neatly. Some people write up their notes like a diary. Some use a loose-leaved book and have a separate page or pages for each bird, such as robin, blackbird, song thrush, and so on. Or you might use a card index for your notes. These are quite cheap to buy and you can have separate cards for different aspects of bird behaviour, such as nest-building, feeding, fighting, preening, and so on, as well as cards for each individual species arranged in alphabetical order.

You may, of course, prefer to keep your bird notes on a computer. Here they can be filed and stored ready for easy access and updating.

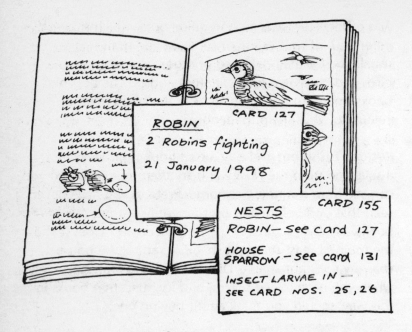

Keeping notes about birds is all part of birdwatching. Even if you never discover any new facts about birds (which is highly unlikely) you will really enjoy looking back over your notebooks and remembering in the years to come places you visited and birds you saw.

They also enable you to swop bird news with friends or share your bird sightings with other members of the Young Ornithologists' Club.

## Binoculars

Once you are really set on becoming a birdwatcher, you will soon want to beg, borrow or buy a pair of binoculars. New or second-hand, binoculars have never been cheaper than they are now, and they are well worth saving up for.

When choosing binoculars, remember the main reason for using them is to make the bird seem larger and nearer. There are many models on the market and it is important to choose the pair which is right for you.

If you look at a pair of binoculars, you will see what looks like a multiplication sum marked on them: 8x30 is a typical example. The first number, in this case 8, shows that the binoculars magnify eight times. Or to put it another way, a bird 80 metres away will appear as if it is only 10 metres away.

The second number, in our example, 30, is the diameter of the objective lenses. These are the lenses furthest away from your eyes when you use the binoculars. The objective lenses control the amount of light passing through the binoculars, and the bigger they are the brighter will be the 'picture' you see through your binoculars.

Binocular magnifications generally range from about x6 – the smallest to be of any real use – to about x12. You might be tempted to go for the highest magnification, but this is a mistake unless you are only interested in sea birds or mountain birds which are usually a long way away. Not only will x12 binoculars be heavy to hold, they won't focus on near objects, and so you might not be able to watch birds at a bird table with them.

## What every birdwatcher needs

For normal daytime use, 8x30, 8x40 or 9x40 binoculars are fine. There are also some small, light binoculars that are 10x24 or 10x30. These will give a better magnification with less weight, but they are not so useful when the weather is dull because they do not let much light through.

Buy the best binoculars you can afford – they will last many years. But whatever binoculars you choose, do try them before you pay for them. Are they comfortable to look through? Do they focus smoothly? Can you hold them steady? Are they too heavy to carry for long periods? Try them in the shop and focus on different objects or, even better, ask to take them outside and focus on advertisements or posters at different distances. Is everything sharp and clear?

To focus a pair of binoculars, look through them at an object which is about 20 metres away. Close your right eye and turn the wheel in the middle of the binoculars until the object is in sharp focus. Now close your left eye and open your right eye. Turn the small wheel on the right eyepiece (this usually has numbers printed on it) until the object is in focus. Then open both your eyes and use your binoculars normally. If you keep the right eyepiece setting the same – perhaps by fixing it with a bit of sticky tape – you only need use the focusing wheel in the middle of the binoculars from now on.

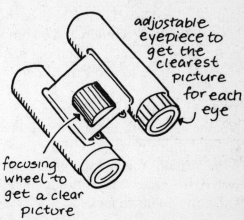

adjustable eyepiece to get the clearest picture for each eye

focusing wheel to get a clear picture

When you use your binoculars, always hang the strap around your neck. Dropping them could mean an expensive repair bill or total loss. Be careful when climbing over stiles that the binoculars don't bang against your body. When you are not using them, return the binoculars to their case and keep them in a dry, clean place. Clean the outside lenses regularly with a special soft lens cleaning tissue or cloth. Don't use harsh scratchy cloth because, although the lenses look hard, they are really quite soft and easily scratched.

Finally, ask your parents if they will insure your binoculars for you. This doesn't cost much and frees you of some of the worries of damaging or losing your binoculars or having them stolen.

# What's that bird?

## Identification

## First steps

You won't get very far as a birdwatcher until you are able to identify the less common and common local birds. With birds, as with people, finding out names is the first step towards getting to know them better.

There is no easy way to becoming an expert birdwatcher. No one expects to become a good tennis-player or pianist without much practice, and the same applies to birdwatching. You will soon find that the more birds you watch, the easier it becomes to identify them, as you get to know the points to look for.

The first thing you need to do is make yourself more observant. Try this little exercise to improve your powers of observation. Go outside with a notebook and pencil. When you see a bird that you know, have a good look at it.

**Did you know?**

*During 1990, Lee Evans, a birdwatcher, recorded 359 different British birds. He travelled nearly 124,000 km to do this.*

10

**Did you know?**

*In 1986, two Kenyan birdwatchers spotted 342 different birds in a 24-hour period.*

When it has gone, make a note of as many of the bird's features as you can. Then go indoors and compare your notes with the picture and description given in your bird book. How many important features did you miss? Would you have been able to identify the bird from your notes alone if you had never seen it before?

Do this several times with birds you can identify, and then try making notes about the birds that you do not know. A park is a good place to start, particularly if it has a lake or pond with gulls or waterfowl, since these birds will be tamer and easier to get close to.

Train yourself to notice as much as you can in a very short time – for often a bird is in view for only a few seconds – and then write down the details about the bird as soon as possible afterwards.

## What's that bird?

Try to make your notes under certain general headings. You may not be able to fill in something under each heading every time, but anything you can note down will help. Here are some of the things you might consider:

## 1 Habitat

The place and type of country (heath, oak wood, lake, pond, etc.) are very important since each bird has its natural habitat. Gannets, razorbills, petrels, puffins and eider ducks, for example, are found only on salt water. Of the land birds, goldcrests, tits, tawny owls, jays and many warblers are never seen in open, treeless country unless they happen to be migrating. On the other hand, starlings, wheatears, rooks, lapwings and short-eared owls always feed out in the open, although starlings and rooks return to trees at night to roost.

Lapwing

Rook

Wheatear

## Did you know?

*The world's smallest bird is the bee hummingbird of Cuba. It is only 6 cm long and weighs less than 2 g.*

## 2 Size of bird

As you'll know how large a sparrow is compared with, say, a town pigeon, you can easily decide whether the unidentified bird is larger or smaller. We might say that a blackbird is halfway between the two or that a swan is much larger than both.

## 3 Shape

A few birds, such as the common wren, are round and small. Sparrow-sized and stout-looking birds include the robin and greenfinch. The wagtails and buntings are all sparrow-sized but slender. Ducks are generally large and plump, and have short tails and long necks.

Wagtail

Greenfinch

Robin

Mallard

Wren

## 4 General colour

What is the bird's main colour? Does it have any patches of colour or stripes on its wings, tail or body? Is its back a different colour from its chest or belly? Does it have eye stripes or chin stripes? If you want to learn the names scientists use for the different parts of the bird's body to help you with your notes, the picture below will be useful.

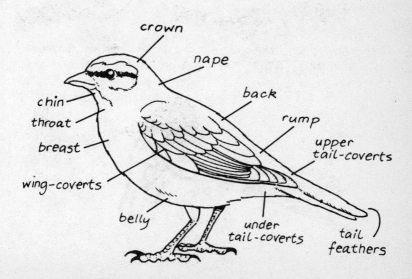

15

# 5 Beak, feet, legs and wings

The shape and colour of these are very important points to note.

## BEAKS

Birds don't have the benefit of knives and forks. Most have to catch and hold their food using only their beaks. As a result, birds' beaks have evolved into many specialist shapes to enable them to tackle different types of food.

*chaffinch*

*Finches have short, stout beaks for cracking seeds.*

*Dunnock*

*Insect-eating birds, such as warblers, tits, flycatchers and treecreepers, usually have rather thin, pointed beaks.*

*Snipe*

*Waders have long, thin beaks for probing for small animals in mud.*

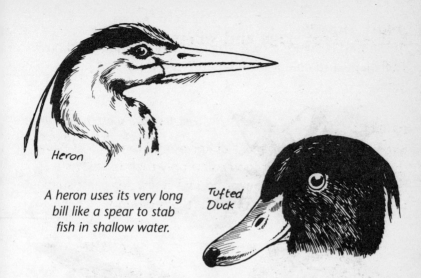

Heron

A heron uses its very long
bill like a spear to stab
fish in shallow water.

Tufted
Duck

A duck has a flat beak for
taking tiny animals and seeds
from the water.

Kestrel

Tawny Owl

Hawks, owls, eagles and other birds of prey have
short, hooked beaks for tearing meat.

17

## WING SHAPES

If the bird is flying, look at the shape of its wings and how it flies.

*Finches have short, broad wings for flitting from tree to tree.*

chaffinch

Swift

*A swift has narrow, swept-back wings for swooping through the air.*

An eagle has long, broad wings for soaring on thermals (rising currents of air).

Golden Eagle

A gull has straight, narrow wings for soaring and gliding over the sea.

Herring Gull

## Did you know?

Swifts spend almost their whole life flying. They land only to lay eggs and to look after their young.

## What's that bird?

### FEET AND LEGS
The shape of a bird's feet and legs are also made for the way it lives.

*House sparrows and most small perching birds have three toes pointing forwards, and a small toe which points backwards.*

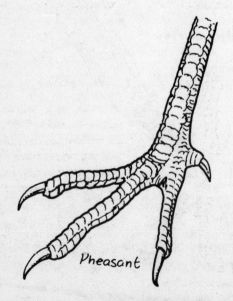

*Ground birds such as pheasants, have strong, thick toes for scratching the soil.*

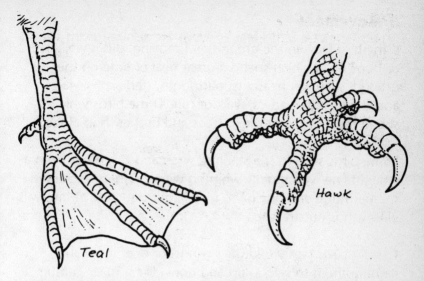

Teal

Hawk

Water birds, such as ducks, geese, swans and gulls, have webbed feet for paddling through water.

Eagles, hawks, owls and other birds of prey use their sharp talons for grasping their prey.

Woodpecker

Tree climbers, such as woodpeckers, use their long toes and claws to grip tree trunks. (Woodpeckers have two toes pointing forwards and two pointing backwards.)

## 6 Movement

If the bird was on the ground and moving, did it walk, run or hop? Birds which spend a great deal of time on the ground, such as pheasants, partridges, starlings, skylarks and the various waders, walk or run. Those birds which spend most of their time in trees and bushes, hop along.

Some birds such as the starling, wren and kingfisher fly in a straight line with rapidly whirring wings. Others, including the partridge and pheasant, fly straight but glide at intervals with wings outstretched.

Certain birds partly fold their wings for brief intervals, causing them to swoop up and down like a roller-coaster. Woodpeckers, the jay and the little owl do this. The largest British birds such as the heron and the mute swan flap their wings slowly as they fly in a straight line, as if flying were hard work – as indeed it often is in bad weather.

On the opposite page, you can see the contrasting flight paths of three British birds.

*The flight paths of a starling, woodpecker and swan*

## 7 Call-notes and song

Any sound you hear the bird make will help you to identify it. Unfortunately, it is not easy to describe bird song in words. It takes time and experience to recognise it, but if you have a good sense of rhythm and an ear for music, it is not a difficult skill to learn, particularly if you can listen to a tape or CD of bird calls.

See over for what a page from your notebook might look like:

Treecreeper

slender
curved beak

brown with
streaks

large
feet

whitish
underside

Size: Slightly smaller than a sparrow.

Shape: Fairly streamlined.

General colour: Back mainly brown with streaks and mottling. Undersides whitish. Wings had pale brown bars.

Beak and legs: Beak slender and curved downwards. Legs brown. Feet quite large for such a small bird.

Movement: Looked like a mouse as it ran up the trunk of a tree. Moved rapidly and jerkily. Seemed to be using its tail like a shooting-stick to support its body.

Call-notes: High pitched 'cheep cheep'.

Habitat: Oak tree, Kensington Gardens, London.

Weather: Cold and frosty, but sunny.

Date and place: London. 1st January 1998.

**What's that bird?**

The next step is to look through your bird book to see which species fits the details in your notes. Start by looking at the pictures. There are not many small birds with such drab colours, but perhaps the most unusual feature is the slender curved bill. When you have narrowed it down to two or three birds, read what the book has to say about each species. These details do in fact identify the bird as a treecreeper, which is the only small brown bird that climbs trees in a mouse-like way.

Do not be discouraged if at first you do not succeed in spotting the all-important features before the bird disappears. Keep looking, try to get closer next time, and eventually, after a bit of practice, you will have no problems in identifying most birds. It's also a great help to go out with an experienced birdwatcher.

# How to get closer

You have to be fairly cunning to get close to some birds. Although birds have a poor sense of smell, they have marvellous eyesight and hearing. A bird of prey, such as an eagle, can see a mouse, eight times further away than we would be able to. We cannot hear worms moving underground or grubs boring deep inside a rotting tree trunk, but some birds can.

**Did you know?**

*A kestrel can spot a small beetle from 30 metres away.*

It is often better to remain still and quiet and wait for the birds to come to you rather than go rushing after them. The small birds that feed in hedgerows, for example, generally work their way along a hedge. So if you stand against the hedge some distance in front of them, they will probably move towards you. Many small birds seem to have difficulty in recognising large objects when they are near to them. To a small bird, you are a large object, and if you stay perfectly still the bird may not notice you. As soon as you move, the bird will spot you and fly off.

*How to make yourself invisible*

## What's that bird?

If the birds won't come to you, you must go nearer to them, always moving quietly and carefully. Use whatever cover is available. Try to keep a hedge, bank, wall, tree trunk, bush or boulder between you and the bird. If you can't walk behind these objects, keep in front of them so that the bird doesn't see you outlined against the sky.

If possible, wear dull coloured clothes for birdwatching. What looks good in the high street can send the birds rushing away in fear. Olive-green, khaki or light brown is much less conspicuous than white, yellow or bright red or blue. Try to avoid the type of waterproof clothing that rustles every time you move.

*The right and wrong way to use a tree when birdwatching*

If you have to cross open ground to get a better view of a bird, do it very slowly. If the ground isn't wet or muddy, and if you are wearing old clothes, do an army crawl, moving along on your elbows and knees.

If you are walking in places where you cannot move quietly, perhaps where there is gravel or a thick carpet of dead leaves, it helps to approach the bird from down-wind, i.e. with the wind blowing in your face. Then the noise you make is carried away from the bird.

Even without binoculars, a skilled birdwatcher can usually get a good view of any bird because he or she is able to guess what it is going to do next, and can use this knowledge to get within a few metres of it. Remember, never go birdwatching alone, after dark, or without an adult's permission.

# Creating a hide

One advantage of studying the birds around your house is that you already have a comfortable hide from which to watch: one of the windows of your home. You could also use the windows of a garage or garden shed to give you a closer look at the birds. If your parents agree, you may be able to screen a window with paper, as shown in the picture.

WINDOW

BLACK PAPER

OBSERVATION HOLE

If you have a large garden, or if you wish to study birds in the country or on a piece of waste ground, it's fun to build a makeshift hide. Then you can get close to birds simply by hiding from them and waiting. You can use an old tent or you can make a kind of small camp from wood and branches. Don't forget to tell an adult what you are up to. They may have some brilliant ideas on how to make a hide too! You should also ask permission if you want to build a hide on someone else's land.

There is no need to camouflage the hide for the bird's sake, but you may have to if it is likely to attract unwanted human attention. A piece of netting through which you weave small leafy twigs works well.

When you go into the hide, it is always best to go with a friend who then departs. This is because birds don't seem to be able to count even up to two, and when your friend leaves they will think that you have gone as well. A small folding stool or a wooden box will enable you to sit in comfort, while a small torch will let you see your notebook or sketchpad.

From your hide you will see many new aspects of bird behaviour. But whenever you are observing birds, be careful not to attract cats, grey squirrels, egg collectors or other pests to their nests. Remember, being a birdwatcher is all about helping to protect birds and their habitats.

# In the picture
## Sketching and photography

## Sketching

'But I never could draw!' you're probably saying. It doesn't matter. This chapter is not how to become a do-it-yourself Leonardo da Vinci or an accomplished bird artist like C. F. Tunnicliffe, but how to make rapid sketches that are useful in describing birds and their behaviour. As they say, a picture is worth a thousand words!

This drawing shows a bird as many of us might draw it.

What's wrong with it? Why has it 'come out the wrong shape'? The answer is that it began with the wrong structure.

What do you think of when you see an egg? Hopefully, a bird! And it's egg shapes we need to draw when we begin to sketch a bird.

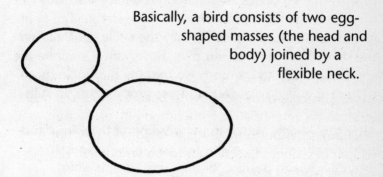

Basically, a bird consists of two egg-shaped masses (the head and body) joined by a flexible neck.

For practice, begin by drawing a large oval. Then try to turn this into a bird. Draw the head in front of the first shape, at the correct spot, and then add the bird's neck and shoulders in a shapely manner.

## In the picture

Taper the rear of the body into a tail, remembering to 'streamline' it into the right position. And now for the legs. They are not just stuck inside the body like two matchsticks! Instead the leg-bones reach a long way into the body until they meet the main framework of the skeleton. The joint just under the bird's body is really the ankle joint, placed the same way round as our own ankle joint. Continue the legs at an angle to the body, so that the bird looks as though it is well balanced, and not propped up on stilts.

After this, simply sketch in the position of the wings and feet and the outlines of the feathers, playing special attention to the position of the 'wrist' of the wings.

*Simple sketch of a bird*

**Did you know?**

*The world's largest bird is the ostrich. It is 2.5 metres high and weighs 150 kilograms.*

Examining birds' skeletons in a museum will help you with your sketching. Study them and see *how* the lines are made and you will learn a lot. It's helpful to sketch from photographs, because here you are really sketching a picture from life. By doing this you will learn much about light and shade and the way birds stand or move.

If you find it too difficult or too slow to make sketches of birds from life, don't worry. You could trace several copies of an outline drawing of a bird in your notebook. Then when you see a 'new' bird, you can simply write into the drawing the bird's colours and how it differs from your outline, e.g. 'longer neck', 'long, slender beak' or 'longer legs'. Then, when you get home, you can look the bird up and colour it in accurately.

**Did you know?**

*The smallest British bird, the goldcrest, needs to eat all day in winter just to have enough energy to stay alive through the night.*

# Photographing birds

Many birdwatchers like to take photographs of the various bird habitats and of the birds that live in them. It is a good way of adding to the information in your notebooks and records.

In order to photograph a bird, you have to be able to get close to it. A bird photographer uses two methods to do this. One is to wait with a camera in a hide, near a bird table, drinking pool or song-post until a bird arrives. The second method is to stalk the bird using a camera with a telephoto or zoom lens.

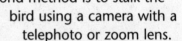

Your average camera used to photograph members of your family and holiday scenes is not usually suitable for taking pictures of smaller birds. Even if you could get close to a bird, the picture of it would still be very small. Do not be put off, though, as these cameras are ideal for taking pictures of the larger birds, such as ducks, geese and swans, and also for photographing bird habitats, including lakes, cliffs, heathland, moors, woodland, and so on.

The best kind of camera for bird photography is the 35mm single lens reflex camera fitted with a zoom or telephoto lens. Such cameras are reasonably light for their size and can be easily carried around. Their biggest advantage, however, is that they have a viewfinder which opens out into the lens at the front of the camera. So, when you look into the viewfinder, you see exactly what the camera lens is seeing.

It takes patience and experience to produce pleasing photographs. Begin by taking general views of the habitats of birds and other related subjects, including trees, flowers, your friends bird-watching, and so on. All this will give valuable practice in using your camera and film.

You can then progress to larger birds and finally to the trickier business of photographing small birds. The best time to try and get a picture of them is when they are feeding at a bird table or in a local park. Happy snapping!

# What's for dinner?

## Bird tables and feeders

The easiest way to start finding out more about local birds is to put food out for them on a bird table. Over 100 species of birds are known to visit bird tables in Britain. You will have no trouble in enticing pigeons, starlings, house sparrows and other common birds. But you will probably be surprised by how many other birds, some normally rare or shy, come for the food you provide. And, in cold weather, you will have the satisfaction of knowing that you are probably saving some birds from starvation – and death.

Here are ten of the most common town or garden birds that may visit your bird table.

robin

wren

starling

great tit

blue tit

# What's for dinner?

chaffinch

house sparrow

jackdaw

*wood pigeon*

*black-headed gull*

# Buying a bird table

You can buy a really expensive bird table with a roof and perches. But such luxury isn't really necessary. The birds are used to eating in the rain and if the table has too many fancy bits, the birds may think it's a trap.

# Make your own bird table

You can easily make your own bird table, even if you're not much good at carpentry! You only need to be able to knock a couple of nails through a piece of wood. It's probably a good idea to ask an adult to help, though.

A rectangle of wood about 30 cm by 45 cm is ideal for a bird table, but anything about that size will do. Nail it to the top of a post about 2 metres long. Put the bird table where you can see it easily, but remember to avoid bushes and trees where cats may lurk. You don't want to give them a tasty meal of one of our feathered friends! If you can, fix a strip of wood about 1 cm wide and 1 cm thick around the edge of the table to stop the food being blown off. Also, leave a gap at each corner to let the rain drain away.

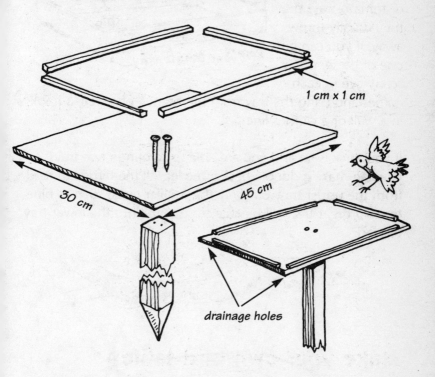

1 cm x 1 cm

30 cm

45 cm

drainage holes

If you'd like an instant table, you could find an old tea tray and fix it to a post (or on a windowsill if you haven't got cats!), to make a bird table. Don't forget to make a few drainage holes in the tray so that the water can drain away in wet weather.

# Bird tables for free

Did you know that
greengrocers often
give away bird
tables? Of course,
they don't really,
but they may have
old wooden potato
or tomato trays that
they usually throw
away. If you can get
one of these, put a
screw eye in each
corner and hang the tray from the branch of a tree, a hook
in a wall or a clothes line.

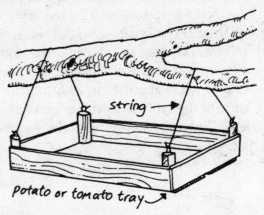

If your luck is in, and you are able to scrounge two trays,
you can make a double-decker feeder. All the birds can feed
from the upper tray, but only the smaller ones, such as blue
tits and great tits, will be able to squeeze into the lower tray
to feed.

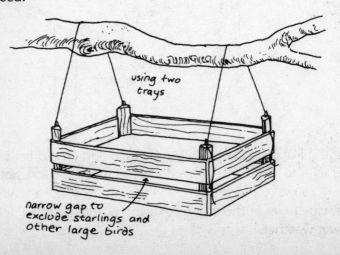

And if you really are no good at woodwork, here is a simple bird table you can make. All you need is a piece of wood and two identical wire or plastic coat hangers. You can hang this bird table from a clothes line or perhaps even the railing on a balcony. If it's windy, use sticky tape to fix the straight sides of the hangers to the wood.

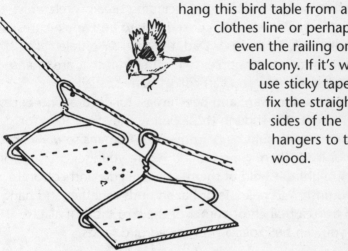

# Looking after your bird table

Once you start feeding the birds, try to keep on doing it. They will come looking for food every day. Winter, when the ground is frozen and insects are scarce, is when birds need extra food.

Make sure the bird table is clean before you put new food on it. If there are stale food or droppings on it, wear gloves and scrape these into the dustbin. Use warm, soapy water to wash the table top, and rinse it and let it dry before adding new food.

# Which foods?

What kinds of food should you put on your table? Almost all kitchen scraps are suitable, including bread (preferably brown), cake, fat, cheese, cooked potato and apple cores. If you talk nicely to Mum or Dad, they can save stale cakes and bread for you or apples and other fruit that are 'going off'. In the autumn you can collect berries, such as hawthorn and rowan, and beech mast for seed-eating birds. Don't forget that though these berries may be a treat for the birds, they could be poisonous for humans so *don't eat them* or leave them lying around where younger brothers or sisters might get hold of them. Use a needle and cotton to thread unshelled peanuts or bacon rinds together and hang them from a branch or corner of the bird table. If all else fails, you can buy specially prepared bird foods.

A word of warning: Buy your peanuts from a reputable supplier. There have been several cases of birds being poisoned by cheap peanuts. And it's best to stop feeding peanuts to the birds during the spring and summer and switch to seeds instead.

### Did you know?

*Many birds that feed on plants swallow small stones and grit to help their bodies grind up the plant material.*

## Did you know?

*The world's least fussy feeder is probably the North American ruffed grouse. Scientists have discovered that this bird will eat at least 518 kinds of animals and 414 different plants.*

# Keep watch

Watch the birds as they visit your bird table. You'll soon discover which birds like to eat at the table, which prefer to picnic on the food which falls to the ground, and what kinds of foods the birds can't resist. Keep a week by week record of which bird species come to your bird table. Look carefully at your results from time to time. Are the birds' feeding habits affected by the weather? Do more birds visit when it is hot or cold, sunny or cloudy, rainy or dry?

You can now become a bit more scientific. Keep the bird table well stocked with food and try to find out whether birds have certain 'meal times'. To do this, record the number of birds of each kind visiting the table during periods of, say, 10 minutes of every hour during the morning and afternoon. Are there times when more birds visit the table than others? Can you find out why this is?

# Where do birds feed?

It is useful to know where and what natural foods a bird eats. Some birds such as blackbirds and house sparrows feed widely. Others such as goldfinches and wrens are much more selective. Choose a species to study.

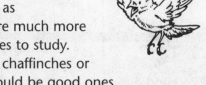

Blackbirds, robins, chaffinches or starlings would be good ones to start with. Work in a park, garden or the school grounds. Make a copy of the chart opposite. Each time you see your chosen species feeding, put a tick in the appropriate column of the table.

| Feeding Areas | Bird species | Blackbird | | | | | | |
|---|---|---|---|---|---|---|---|---|
| Open grass | ✔ | | | | | | | |
| Flower beds | | | | | | | | |
| In trees | | | | | | | | |
| Below trees | | | | | | | | |
| Under shrubs | ✔ | | | | | | | |
| Berries on shrubs | | | | | | | | |
| Compost heaps | | | | | | | | |
| Bird table | | | | | | | | |
| Other | | | | | | | | |

Can you find out what the bird is eating? Where does your chosen bird species feed most often?

49

# Who's the boss?

You will probably notice that, rather like little children at a birthday party, the birds squabble over the food you provide, even though there's plenty for everyone.

Some birds will chase others off the bird table. A few which normally find their own food will turn to robbery if they get the chance. A mistle thrush, for example, will often make the smaller song thrush drop the food it has collected. Sometimes the food will change hands – or rather beaks – several times before it is finally swallowed.

Keep records of all cases of this type of bullying and robbery – scientists call it 'dominance'. Gradually you will build up a list of such behaviours and be able to work out the bird that is regularly chased away or robbed, but which never succeeds in retaliating. You will also discover the bully that always chases other birds off, or steals their food, but is itself never robbed or chased. Bullies include blackbirds, starlings, song thrushes and greenfinches. Victims include house sparrows, wrens, blue tits and coal tits. Can you discover others?

Another way to set out your results is on a diagram like this. The arrows point from each dominant bird towards its victim. Where there are parallel arrows, it means the 2 birds are sometimes the bullies and sometimes the victims in confrontations with each other.

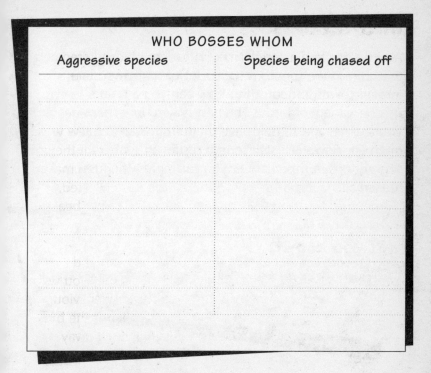

| WHO BOSSES WHOM | |
|---|---|
| Aggressive species | Species being chased off |
| | |
| | |
| | |
| | |
| | |
| | |
| | |

You can depict your results as a diagram.

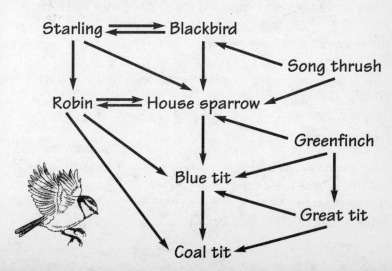

# Bird feeders

A bird table and a sprinkling of breadcrumbs and seeds on the ground are sure to attract a lot of sparrows, starlings and, in towns, pigeons. But how can you attract an even greater variety of birds? The best way to lure them near your home, and to help save them from starvation, is to open your own self-service bird restaurant! With the suggestions in this chapter, you can satisfy the fussiest feeders.

## Did you know?

*The greedy Egyptian vulture breaks open ostrich eggs, to eat the contents, by dropping stones onto them.*

All the bird feeders described in this chapter are easy to make and they won't cost you much since they're all made from junk. You don't need a garden because you can hang them almost anywhere outside – including on walls, fences, windowsills, window boxes, balconies or clothes lines, as well as from trees and bird tables. Between them, these feeders are guaranteed to tempt even the daintiest diners. And you can also use them to find out more about the feeding behaviour of birds.

# A net bag feeder

Many small birds love peanuts – but not the salted kinds, as *these can kill*. You can buy a container to use for nuts and seeds but a good, cheap substitute is the small plastic net bags in which nuts and oranges are sold.

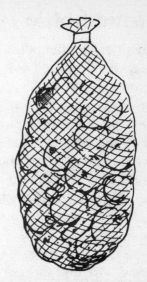

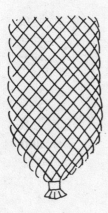

Neatly cut one end off the bag and remove the contents, taking care not to tear the bag. Fill with peanuts, sunflower seeds or other bird food.

Tie the top with string and hang the bag from the underside of the bird table or from the branch of a tree.

# Plastic bottle feeders

Find an old washing-up liquid bottle. Wash it out thoroughly and then carefully remove the top. Ask an adult to help you cut off the stopper with scissors. Pass string through the top and tie a knot in it. Then, again with an adult, carefully cut four slits about 0.5 cm wide down the bottle with a sharp knife or scissors. Use thin sticks or old pencils for perches. Make some small holes in the bottom to let rainwater out. Fill the feeder with peanuts or sunflower seeds and hang it up where you can see it from a window.

Remove the top of a washing up liquid bottle. Using scissors, remove the stopper.

Pass string through top. Fill bottle with food and replace top.

Hang up the bottle in a suitable place.

Using a sharp knife carefully cut four slits (0.5 cm wide) down the bottle.

Place these at regular intervals around bottle.

slits

Use thin sticks or pencils as perches.

Small holes to allow rainwater to drain.

A clean plastic lemonade bottle or a fabric softener bottle also makes a good feeder. Ask an adult to help you cut two round holes in the side of the bottle with sharp scissors. Make a hole in the lid so that you can hang it up. Put food in the bottom of the bottle.

# Bottle top feeders

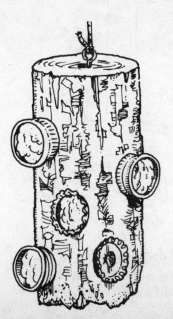

Don't throw away metal bottle tops. Instead, take a short piece of wood and nail several tops along it. Make sure there are no sharp corners which could injure birds. Put a screw eye in one end of the piece of wood. Fill the bottle tops with fat and hang up your feeder.

# Lantern style bird feeders

If there is still anything left in the rubbish bin, here's another easy-to-make feeder!

You will need a large and smaller aluminium foil pie dish, a stick about 15 cm long and the thickness of a broom handle and two jar lids.

Ask an adult to make a small hole for you in the centre of each jar lid. Then carefully put a drawing pin or short screw through the hole in one lid, through the smaller pie dish and into the end of the stick. (The jar lid should have its opening facing downwards.)

string or wire

jar lid

stick

aluminium foil pie dish

bird food

smaller foil pie dish

jar lid

nail

Now put a screw through the centre of the larger pie dish, through the hole in the other jar lid, and into the other end of the stick. Again the lid should be facing downwards. Hang your feeder from a tree branch, balcony or clothes line, using string or wire, and put some food in the lower dish.

# Pine cone feeders

What about a bit of simple cooking? Collect some large pine cones. Then ask an adult to help you melt 50 gm of lard in a saucepan and leave it on one side to cool.

Stir in 25 gm of peanut butter together with a large table-spoon of plain flour.

When the mixture is cool, but still runny, use a table knife to fill all the crannies in the pine cones with it.

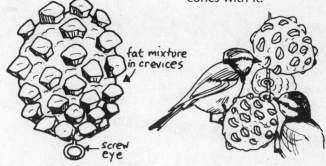

fat mixture in crevices

screw eye

Put a screw-eye into the base (the wide part) of each pine cone, and then hang them from a branch or the under-side of the bird table.

When the pine cones are empty they can be washed in warm, soapy water, rinsed in clean water, dried and refilled with more of the mixture.

If you can't find any pine cones, you can always put the fatty mixture in bottle tops, as described on page 55.

# Bird puddings

For a special treat, perhaps at Christmas or when there is cold, snowy weather, why not make the birds a pudding? Along with an adult's help you will need a spoon, a small basin and some fat or suet. You will also need as many of the following bird foods as possible: seeds and nuts, sultanas or currants, brown bread crumbs and scraps of cheese.

Half fill the basin with a mixture of the bird foods and then stir in the same amount of melted fat or suet. (Ask an adult to help you melt these.) You can either leave the mixture to set solid in the basin, and then turn it out on the bird table or, while the mixture is still sticky, spoon it lightly into a coconut shell or small flowerpot and hang it up outside. The birds will flock to it!

### Did you know?

*When an ostrich at London Zoo died, it was found to have eaten an alarm clock, 91 cm of rope and a small collection of coins.*

# Keep records

Watch carefully to see which birds visit your feeders. See how they take the food. Do they peck off little bits, or do they take large lumps and fly off with them? Keep notes as to which birds seem to prefer which feeders and which foods.

# Which foods do birds like best?

For this investigation you will need a small plank of wood and five or six jar or can lids.

Place your lids equal distances apart on the plank and nail or glue them in place with an adult's help. Put the plank on the ground where you can see it clearly, but away from trees and bushes where cats and other predators might lurk.

Put equal amounts of a different food in each lid. Try breadcrumbs, fat, bacon rind, seeds, cheese or cooked potato, for example.

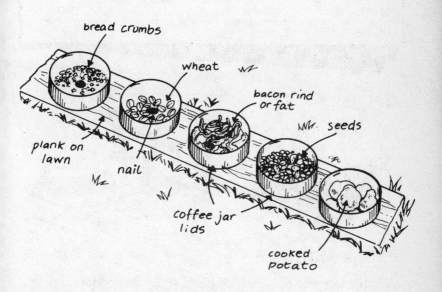

bread crumbs

wheat

bacon rind or fat

seeds

plank on lawn

nail

coffee jar lids

cooked potato

Watch carefully to see which kind of bird eats what food. Which lid is emptied first?

## What's for dinner?

It would be a good idea to make a record of your findings like the one shown below. Also you could experiment with more foods. You might, for example, try putting a different kind of seed in each container, such as sunflower seeds, rape seeds, mustard and cress seeds, wheat, oats or barley. Do all birds have the same favourite food?

| Bird | Food | | | | |
| --- | --- | --- | --- | --- | --- |
| | bread-crumbs | fat | wheat seeds | cheese | cooked potato |
| House sparrow | ✗ | | ✗ | | |
| Starling | ✗✗ | ✗ | ✗ | ✗✗ | ✗✗✗ |
| Robin | | | | | |

# Milk carton feeders

It's easy to turn milk cartons into feeders. Mark an opening on a clean milk carton with a ballpoint pen, and then cut it out carefully with scissors. Close the top of the carton and make a small hole right through it with the point of the scissors. Thread a large paperclip through this hole and hang up the carton. Put a handful of peanuts or bird seed in the feeder and see which birds visit it.

Once the birds have got used to your first milk carton feeder, make some more. But this time cut holes of all different shapes and sizes. Put the same kind of food in each feeder, to make your experiment fair, and hang them up in a row.

## What's for dinner?

Keep a record of how many birds of each kind visit each feeder. What is the most popular design for the feeder? If you do the experiment again, with the favourite carton in a different position in the line, do you still get the same result?

Now make some more milk carton feeders of the most popular design. This time paint each one a different colour using modeller's enamel paint or emulsion paint. Let the paint dry and then put the same kind of food in each feeder and hang them up in a line. Keep a record of how many birds of each kind visit each colour feeder. Which colour feeder do the birds like best?

# 5 Who's a clever boy?

## Testing birds' intelligence

When people are being rude, they sometimes say someone is a 'bird-brain'. But are birds really so dumb? Here are some simple experiments you can do to find out how intelligent birds are when it comes to finding food.

If they come across something new, most birds play safe and don't go too near it, at first. The exceptions are the tits which are always amongst the first to investigate possible new foods. Their habit of pecking at the tops of milk bottles to reach the cream inside is a good example.

# Who's a clever boy?

Before you can begin your experiments, you have to get the birds used to feeding in one place, such as a bird table. Then hide a pinch of food under a rectangle of card folded down the middle to form a tent. Or, cover the food with the upturned tray of a matchbox. Sprinkle a few breadcrumbs around the tent or matchbox to attract the birds, and watch carefully to see what happens.

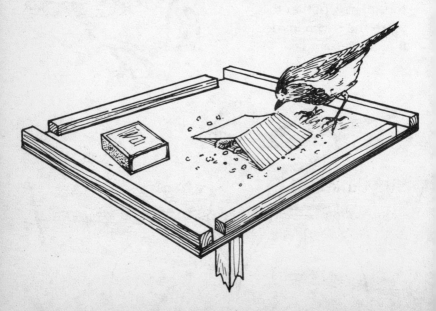

Next, cover a little food with an upturned small jar, such as a meat or fish paste jar. Now the birds can see the food, but they can't get to it easily. Do any of the birds reach the food? If so, how?

Yellowhammer investigating food under an upturned jam jar.

### Did you know?

*The woodpecker finch of the Galapagos Islands uses a cactus spine to hook insect grubs out of holes in wood.*

## Who's a clever boy?

Now try something different. For two or three days, put out a string of peanuts (remember, *not* salted peanuts), or hang up a small piece of suet or bacon rind. When the birds are used to feeding from the string of food, hang it inside a wide-necked clear plastic bottle. You may have to put a few pebbles in the bottom of the bottle to stop it blowing over. Do the birds reach the food? If so, how do they do it?

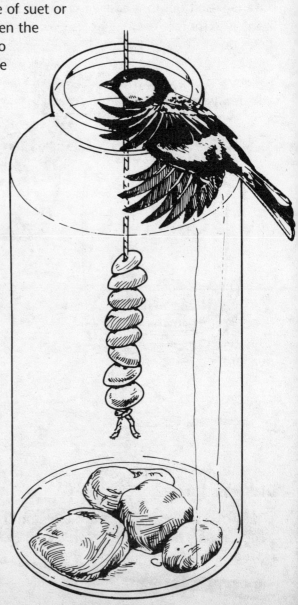

For a harder intelligence test, find a piece of transparent plastic tubing about 15 cm long which is sealed up at one end. One of the tubes in which toothbrushes are sold is ideal. Make a row of small holes about 3 cm apart along one side of the tube by carefully pushing and twisting a nail into it. The holes should be large enough for a matchstick to move in and out easily. At the open end of the tube, cut a larger hole about 1 cm in diameter.

Take a small piece of board and fix the plastic tube to it with plasticine or Blu-tack. Put a matchstick in the lower hole of the plastic tube and rest an unsalted peanut on it.

Stand your apparatus out on the bird table, sprinkle some crumbs around it, and then see how long it is before the birds discover it. Is any bird able to get the peanut by pulling out the matchstick? What kind of bird is it?

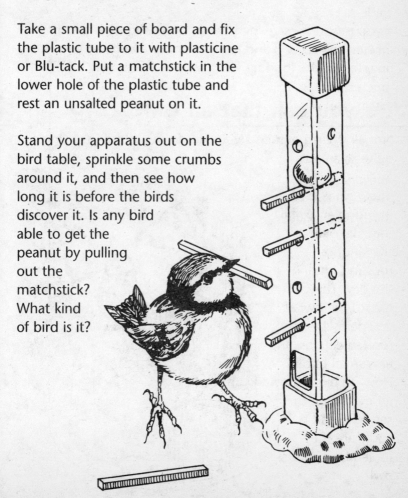

### Who's a clever boy?

Now make the test harder still by putting two matchsticks in the tube, with the peanut resting on top of the upper matchstick. A bird now has to pull out both matchsticks to get the peanut. If a bird manages this, put matchsticks in all the small holes in the tube, with the peanut resting on the very top one. A bird boffin will have to pull out all the matchsticks before it can get a peanut. Is any bird clever enough to work this out?

If you repeat these experiments, how long does the bird take on the second and later attempts? Do other birds learn how to get the food by watching the first brainy ones?

## Do you call that an owl?

Not all the experiments you can do show birds as being quite so smart.

Many small birds will mob an owl if they discover it sleeping, or roosting, during the day. They regard the owl as an enemy because it often catches and eats small birds. How do birds know an owl when they see one, and how easily are they fooled by a model owl?

Make a model tawny owl, using a jar about 20 cm high and 8 cm in diameter. Mix up some paste by stirring plain flour into a little cold water until you have a sticky mixture. Then tear a newspaper into strips about 2 cm wide.

Turn the jar upside down and cover it with two or three layers of newspaper strips that have been wetted with clean water. Then add several layers of newspaper strips wetted with glue or paste.

When it has dried a little, carefully slide the model off the jar. Trim the bottom and paint one section of the side (the front of the bird) very light brown. Paint the rest dark brown.

Stand the model owl outside in the open on a wall, post or branch, where both you and the birds can see it. Sprinkle some breadcrumbs on the ground around the model. Do small birds take any notice of the model owl?

## Who's a clever boy?

Now trace the owl's face shown below on to a piece of paper or thin card and cut it out. Glue the face on to the model owl in the correct position.

Do small birds take any notice of the 'improved' model? If so, what kinds of birds are they and what do they do?

## Did you know?

*Owls have such huge eyes that there isn't room to move them in their sockets. Instead they can turn their whole head to look to the side or even behind them.*

If you can, make more model owls of different sizes but all the same colour as before. Test them one at a time. What effect do they have? You could also try model owls that are all the same size but different colours, such as red, black and green. Do the birds take any notice of these?

*Caution:* Do not leave the model owls in place for a long time, and do not do this activity when the birds are nesting, since you may make parent birds desert their eggs or young. And it is not fair to carry out this activity in very cold weather when you might prevent birds that are starving hungry from feeding.

# Song thrushes and snails

Song thrushes eat a lot of snails. They take a snail to a stone, often called the thrush's anvil, and break the snail shell on the stone, so that they can eat the animal inside. You can tell a thrush's anvil by the heap of snail shells around it.

Carefully watch a thrush at its anvil. Does it hold the shell and crack it the same way every time? Make a collection of the shells from around the anvil and try to find out from a reference book what kind of snails they are.

Thrushes often take empty shells to their anvils without realising they are empty – until they begin to swing them towards the stone. It never seems to occur to the thrush that the shell it is carrying is too light to have anything in it. Find some empty snail shells, pack them with differing amounts of clay or plasticine, and leave them on a lawn or path where thrushes can see them.

How do the thrushes react to the artificial snails? If a snail shell is too heavy for the thrush to carry, what does it do?

# Warning colours

Small animals that are poisonous, harmful or nasty-tasting are often brightly coloured. Ladybirds, wasps and the black-and-yellow striped caterpillars of the cinnabar moth are good examples. Birds soon learn by experience to avoid these creatures.

Most birds will eat moist brown bread but dislike the taste of vinegar. Cut out two pieces of cardboard each about 7 x 7 cm. Colour one with red and white stripes, the other with black and yellow stripes. Soak a slice of brown bread in water and lay it on the ground with the red and white card on it. Soak a second slice of brown bread in vinegar and lay it on the ground, next to the first piece, with the black and yellow card on it.

## Who's a clever boy?

Watch carefully to see what happens. How soon do the birds learn to avoid the bread with the black and yellow marker? What happens if you replace the bread soaked in vinegar with another piece of bread soaked in water? Do the birds still avoid it?

## Did you know?

*The secretary bird of the African grasslands has hard scales on its long legs to protect them from the poisonous snakes the bird stamps on and eats.*

# Water, water everywhere
## Drinking and bathing

Like us, birds need clean water to drink and to bathe in. Even a small dish of clean water will bring birds flocking in from miles away, especially in built-up areas where there are few puddles and pools in dry weather.

If you don't have much room, a shallow drinking bowl or a large margarine tub will do. It should be at least 10 cm wide and deep enough to hold 2 or 3 cm of water. Change the water every day, and every few days scrub out the container, while wearing gloves, and sterilise it in a weak solution of household disinfectant. Rinse it thoroughly before you refill it
with clean water.

margarine
tub →

Coal
Tit

dustbin lid

If you have a garden, however small, then you can use a bigger container. Choose one that is not too deep and which doesn't have slippery sides, as the birds must be able to get a good grip. An upturned dustbin lid is ideal, but even an old frying pan is better than a fancy bird bath surrounded by gnomes, pixies and plaster frogs. You could also use an old washing-up bowl. Lay the bowl or dustbin lid on the ground with the opening facing downwards. Carefully scratch a line around it with a stick. Dig out the soil inside the circle you have drawn so that the bowl or lid will fit neatly into it. Sink it into the ground before you fill it with water and put a large stone in the middle for the birds to stand on.

## Did you know?

*When danger threatens, a moorhen dives under water. It stays under by gripping a weed with its feet and poking the tip of its beak above water to breathe.*

# Keeping the water from freezing

It is difficult to stop the birds' water from freezing in winter. With ponds and other large areas of water, the only way to keep some open water is to make a hole in the ice. Don't use a hammer for this. Instead, carefully lower the bottom of a hot (not boiling) kettle or saucepan on the ice until it melts. A large rubber ball floating in the water will sometimes prevent the whole surface from freezing over.

Whatever you do, *never* add salt, glycerine, anti-freeze or any other chemical to the water to stop it from freezing. These could poison the birds.

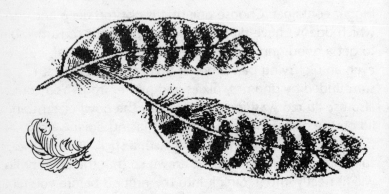

# Drinking behaviour

Make a list of all the bird species that you see drinking from your garden pond or bird bath. Keep notes on how they drink. Some birds seem to sip the water daintily while others tip their heads back when they swallow. Record how often each species drinks and try to relate this to their food. Do seed-eating birds drink more or less often than insect-eaters, for example?

# Bathing behaviour

Even a small bird has at least 2,000 to 3,000 feathers, and these have to be kept clean if the bird is to stay warm and dry and be able to fly.

Keep a record of which birds come to bathe in your pond or bird bath. Make a note of the time of day and the weather conditions, particularly the temperature, when you see birds bathing. Do more birds bathe at certain times of the day? Do birds bathe more when the weather is hot or cold, wet or dry? Do the birds preen immediately after they have bathed? Where do they do this?

## Did you know?

*Some swans have more than 25,000 feathers.*

# Birds on the water

Watch the birds on your local lake or pond. Which birds feed by 'dabbling'? Some birds actually put their heads under the water to feed. This makes them look as though they are standing on their heads. Can you see any of these? Other water birds dive under water to find food. Which species are these?

Using a stop-watch or a watch with a second hand, you can make a study of diving birds. Each time, say, a great-crested grebe or a tufted duck goes under water, time how long its dive lasts. Do this several times for each bird of every species. If you can, work out an average for the different bird species.

Which bird species has the longest average dive? Which has the shortest dive? Investigate these questions in different seasons and compare your results. Does the average length of the dive for each species change?

Why not create a graph like the one opposite to record your findings for each species? This one shows that most tufted ducks dive for between 18 and 24 seconds, but a few stay under for 34 to 36 seconds.

## Did you know?

*Some penguins can swim to a depth of 265 metres under the water.*

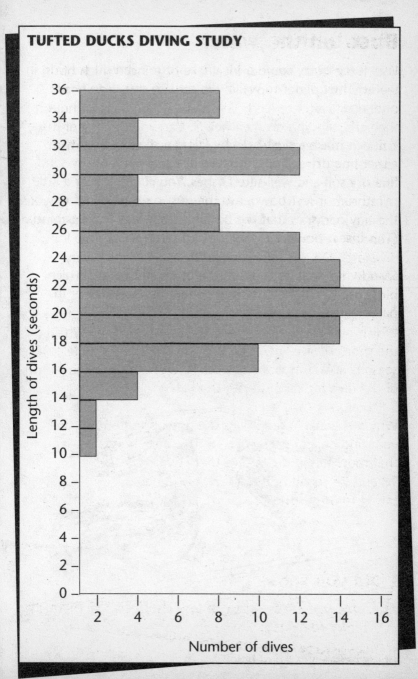

**TUFTED DUCKS DIVING STUDY**

# Dust baths

Like some of us, some birds are not too keen on bathing in water! They prefer to wallow in dust to dry-clean their plumage.

You can make a dust-bath by filling a shallow box with either fine dry soil or a mixture of equal parts of dry sand, fine dry soil and well-sifted ashes. You could scatter a little pyrethrum insect powder in the dust bath to kill off any of the tiny parasites that the bathing birds may leave behind. (This insect powder is safe for birds and pets.)

Stand your dust bath out in the open and record which birds use it. Do they use it at certain times of day or in particular kinds of weather?

*House sparrows in a dust bath*

# Sun-bathing, anting and smoke-bathing

Just as some people like to sun-bathe, so do blackbirds and some other species. Unfortunately we don't know much about this habit. To help us learn more, keep records of the species and numbers of birds you see sun-bathing, together with the place, date and weather conditions. How does the bird sit or lie while it is sun-bathing?

*Blackbird sun-bathing*

Some birds have rather odd habits. Some like to wallow in an ants' nest and let the ants crawl over their feathers. It is thought they do this to help get rid of the tiny parasites that live amongst their feathers. If you do come across an ants' nest, see if any birds use it for this 'anting' behaviour.

## Did you know?

*Crows sometimes pick up glowing cigarette ends or even twigs from bonfires and rub them on their feathers.*

Other birds cavort in the smoke from chimneys and one or two species have been seen 'bathing' in a clump of flowers – perhaps they like the smell!

*Starlings anting*

If you come across any of these strange types of bird behaviour, make careful notes on everything you see. These are the kinds of activities other birdwatchers will be keen to hear about.

# Home, sweet home
## Birds' nests and boxes

Many birds like to nest in holes in old trees. Unfortunately in many parts of Britain there are no longer any suitable old trees. Thousands have been blown down during the severe gales of recent years, and in many places old trees are cut down because they are dangerous. The result is that many small birds have difficulty finding somewhere to nest.

Fortunately, nest-boxes are a good substitute for the holes found in old trees. They are also warm, snug places for the birds to roost in winter. Blue tits and great tits use nest-boxes most commonly, but over 60 kinds of birds have been known to use a box. It is possible to buy ready-made nest-boxes, but it is quite easy to make your own.

## Did you know?

*Sometimes in winter wrens roost together. One nest-box was found to contain 63 sleeping wrens.*

*A robin in St Albans, Hertfordshire, once nested in a motorcyclist's crash helmet.*

*Birds' nest soup is made from the nests of small birds called cave swiftlets that live in caves in Asia.*

# Making a bird nest-box

The box shown here, with a hole in the front, will attract blue tits, coal tits, great tits and other birds that normally nest in holes in trees.

To make the box, you will need a plank of wood 15 cm wide and 145 cm long. (An old piece of floor boarding is ideal.) You will also need small nails, a strip of rubber, two small brass catches and the help of an adult.

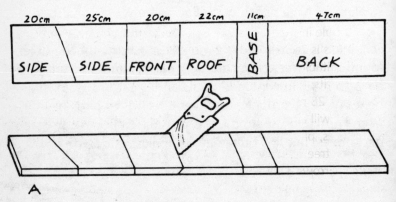

| 20cm | 25cm | 20cm | 22cm | 11cm | 47cm |
|------|------|------|------|------|------|
| SIDE | SIDE | FRONT | ROOF | BASE | BACK |

A

Mark the wood as shown in the picture. Begin by cutting the wood into two pieces with an angled cut. Now make the other cuts so that you finish up with six pieces of wood.

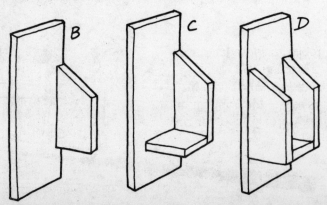

B C D

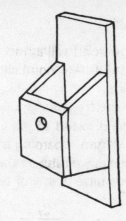

e

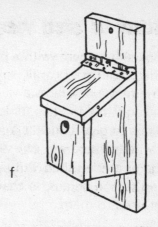

f

Draw a hole in the front section. If this is 25 mm in diameter it is suitable for coal, marsh and blue tits; for great tits it should be 28 mm; while a 32 mm hole will also let in nuthatches, pied flycatchers, redstarts, tree sparrows and house sparrows. Drill a few small drainage holes in the floor section of the box. Then nail or screw the sections together.

Nail a strip of rubber (a piece of old tyre inner tube will do) or leather to the lid and back to form a hinge. Fit a catch to each side of the lid. Paint the outside of your nest-box with wood preservative to stop it rotting away, but *don't* use creosote.

For robins, pied wagtails, spotted flycatchers and wrens, make the same box with the upper part of the front cut off so that it is only about 10 cm high.

*Open-fronted nest-box*

# Where to put the box

Ask an adult to help you fix your nest-box 3 to 5 metres up a tree trunk, fence or wall, so that it is out of reach of cats. Make sure the box faces away from direct sun and the prevailing wind and rain, unless there are trees and buildings to give it shelter. You may want to put it somewhere where you can see it easily from your house, garage or garden shed. Put up nest-boxes well before the nesting season begins, so that the birds have plenty of time to get used to them.

# A simple tray nest-box

Even simpler to make is a wooden tray nest-box. Use a small seed tray or the bottom of a wooden cigar box. With an adult's help, drill a few holes in the bottom for drainage and fix it to a tree trunk, wall or fence. Robins, pied wagtails, spotted flycatchers or even blackbirds may use this type of nest-box, particularly if it is tucked away amongst ivy or some other climbing plant. If the tray is fastened high up on a beam or ledge in an outbuilding where a window has been left open, it may be taken over by swallows.

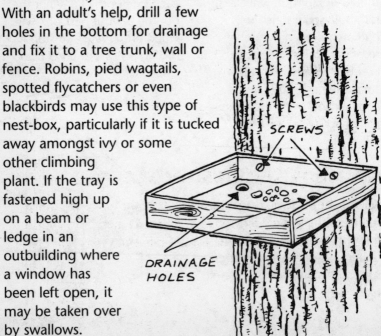

SCREWS

DRAINAGE HOLES

# Keeping watch

Don't touch the box during
the nesting season, but
watch the birds from a safe
distance. The hinged lid of
the box with the nest-hole is only
for cleaning the old nest out in the autumn.

Can you see what nesting materials the adult birds take to
the box? Do one or both birds of the pair build the nest?
What food is taken to the young, and how often? Are the
young fed by one parent or both? Are the young birds able
to fly when they leave the nest-box?

## Did you know?

*The long-tailed tit makes a beautiful domed nest of
moss and lichen which may be lined with up to
2,000 feathers.*

# Cleaning the nest-boxes

Clean the nest-boxes out in the autumn, while wearing
gloves. But leave each for several weeks after any young
birds have left the nest, as for a while they may still come
back to the box to roost.

# A builder's yard for birds

In spring and early summer, birds sometimes have difficulty in finding nesting materials. You can help them by collecting together dried grass, dried moss, scraps of knitting wool cut into short pieces, the combings from horses, dogs or cats, carpet fluff, sheep's wool and chicken feathers. Put them all into a string bag, like those in which onions or Brussels sprouts are sold in supermarkets.

Hang the bag from the strong branch of a tree or from a clothes line or balcony. Push one or more sticks through the lower part of the bag to act as perches.

*Providing nesting materials for birds*

On the ground, near your net bag, put a large old tray filled with wet mud. Watch carefully to see which birds come to your bag. Which nesting materials do the birds seem to like best?

*Warning:* If birds do nest in
your garden or anywhere else,
don't go near them.
The parents may abandon
their eggs or leave their
babies to die if they are
disturbed.

## Did you know?

*A pair of mistle thrushes in Glasgow built their nest on
top of a street light. It must have been warm and
cosy at night!*

# Birds' nests

There is a lot to find out about birds' nests. Do some preliminary work in the spring and summer, by recording the position of any nests that you find and identifying the species to which they belong. You can begin a detailed study in the autumn after the young birds have flown and the nests have been deserted. However, some nests are used by birds and other animals as roosts or hibernation sites in winter, so you must double-check that a nest is not being used.

## Home, sweet home

Before you touch any nest, record its position including, if it is in a tree, the species of the tree and the height of the nest above ground. Then, remove the nest wearing gloves, dust it with pyrethrum insect powder and place it in a large unperforated polythene bag. Seal the bag up and leave it for two or three days. This will kill any parasites that may be lurking. Then take the nest out of the bag and allow it to dry out thoroughly.

insect powder

weigh nest

mosses and lichens

grasses

twigs

feathers

mud

Weigh the nest as accurately as you can and then carefully pull it to pieces. Separate the material into heaps – moss and lichens in one pile, dry grass in another, mud in another, twigs in another, and so on. Weigh or measure the contents of each pile.

You could draw up a table like this to record your findings:

| Nesting material | Weight in grams for each species | | | |
|---|---|---|---|---|
| | Blackbird | Sparrow | Thrush | Blue tit* |
| Dry grass | | | | |
| Moss | | | | |
| Lichens | | | | |
| Feathers | | | | |
| Mud | | | | |
| Leaves | | | | |
| Twigs | | | | |
| Other | | | | |

*These birds are just suggestions for you to study. You can of course choose any species you come across.

Over a period of time, you should be able to compile a list of the favourite nesting materials and favourite nest sites for various species. (See p.115 on how to keep whole nests.)

# A survey of house martins' nests

House martins do seem scarcer these days. Is this true where *you* live?

Make a survey of the house martins' nests in your area. If you have a large-scale map (these can often be obtained free from an estate agent's office), you could mark in the approximate positions of the nests on the map.

There seem to be at least three kinds of house martins' nest: the common type, which is constructed of mud, is built under the eaves of a house or some other building; a second type is built in the point formed by the roof; and another type is built into the corner of a window. How many of each can you find?

Which side of a building do the house martins prefer? Use a compass to find out if the nest is facing north, south, east or west. Do the birds seem to prefer any particular colour paintwork when building nests on houses? Are there more nests on old buildings than on new ones? Where do the martins obtain their supplies of mud? How many of the nests are later taken over by house sparrows? How many nests are knocked down by the owners of houses? Why? Is it because the birds foul the path or step with their droppings? This problem can be overcome quite easily by fitting a shelf just below the nest until the young birds have flown. (It would be illegal for anyone to knock off house martins' nests while they are in use.)

### Did you know?

*House martins used to nest on cliffs. A few still do but most now nest on buildings. A house martin's nest may contain more than 2,500 beakfuls of mud.*

# 8 Birds on the move
## Migration and territories

*Question:* Why do birds fly south in the autumn?
*Answer:* Because it's too far to walk!

Every year millions of birds fly from one part of the world to another. These journeys are called migrations, and birds don't just go jaunting off for the fun of it. They migrate to avoid harsh weather, to find food or to breed. Other birds make smaller journeys. In the winter, for example, starlings and gulls roost together at night in large flocks in places where they feel safe, but in the daytime they spread out in small groups to feed. Similarly, some wading birds which spend the spring and summer inland, fly to coastal marshes for the winter.

### Did you know?

*The Arctic tern migrates further than any other bird. It travels between its winter home in the Antarctic and its breeding ground in the Arctic and back again each year, a journey of about 35,000 km.*

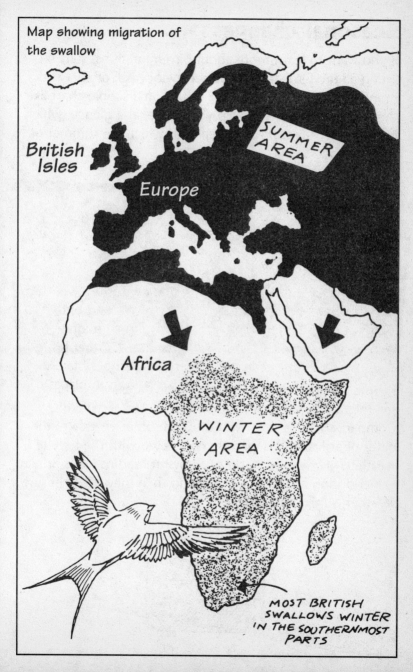

Map showing migration of the swallow

SUMMER AREA

British Isles

Europe

Africa

WINTER AREA

MOST BRITISH SWALLOWS WINTER IN THE SOUTHERNMOST PARTS

# Seasonal changes

If you want to learn more about bird migrations, start by listing all the bird species you see every week or every month for a year. Record your results on a simple chart like the one below. This will help you to see, at a glance, which bird species stay with us all year and which are summer or winter visitors.

| Bird | Jan. | Feb. | Mar. | Apr. | May | Jun. | July | Aug. | Sep. | Oct. | Nov. | Dec. |
|------|------|------|------|------|-----|------|------|------|------|------|------|------|
| Robin | X | X | X | X | X | X | X | X | X | X | X | X |
| Song thrush | X | X | X | X | X | X | X | X | X | X | X | X |
| House martin | – | – | – | X | X | X | X | X | X | X | – | – |

Keep a careful record each year of the dates when you first see migrant bird species and when you last see them. Compare these records with those for other years. Are the dates of arrival and departure connected with the type of weather? For example, do swallows or martins leave Britain earlier during a cold or wet autumn than they do when the weather is mild and sunny?

# Looking for bird rings

To find out about the journeys or migrations made by birds, scientists attach a very light metal ring to the legs of some birds. They may also put coloured rings on birds, so that they can easily recognise individuals whose daily lives they may wish to study.

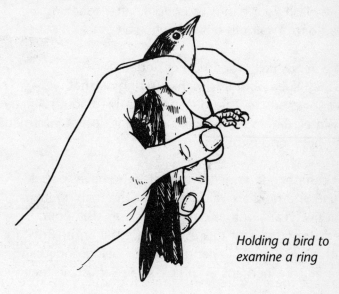

*Holding a bird to examine a ring*

If you come across a bird that has been stunned or injured, look carefully to see if it has a numbered metal ring on one of its legs. If it has, note the number and other writing on the ring if you can and send this information, with details of where and when you found the bird, to The Ringing Department, British Trust for Ornithology, The Nunnery, Thetford, Norfolk, IP24 2PU. If the bird also has coloured rings, note which of the bird's legs they are on and the order of the colours, reading from the top of the bird's leg down to its foot. Send this information to the British Trust for Ornithology too. If the bird is dead, remove the rings and send those as well, but do not try to take the ring off a live bird, since birds' legs break very easily. In any case, the ringed bird may turn up somewhere else later. Eventually you will be sent a history of the bird saying where and when it was ringed. At the same time, you will be helping scientists to find out more about the journeys birds make.

Always wash your hands thoroughly after touching a dead bird. Wear old gloves if you can.

Only a very small proportion of ringed birds are ever seen again, but it is thanks to ringing that we know, for example, that our swallows fly to South Africa for the winter. Ringing also gives us a great deal of information about how long birds live.

Birds can only be ringed by people who have special training and hold an official licence. The training takes about five years, but you may be able to visit a bird observatory (for your nearest, contact the British Trust for Ornithology, see p.117) and see birds being ringed and, if you are lucky, perhaps even help the scientists in their work.

### Did you know?

*The ancient Greeks tied coloured threads around the legs of migrating swallows to try to find out where they spent the winter.*

# A bird song diary

It takes practice to be able to identify the different bird
songs. The easiest way to learn them is to go out with an
experienced birdwatcher, or buy a tape or CD and listen to
that. If not, stick to the common bird species and record
only those you actually see singing.

Some species, like the cuckoo, sing for only a very short
time. Others, like the blackbird, sing for much longer.
However long the bird sings, it is usually bragging
something along the lines of 'I am a handsome male
blackbird. I own this territory. Other males, keep away!
Female blackbirds come closer!'

Keep a diary of the birds you hear singing near your home
or school. Each month enter your findings in a summary
chart like the one below.

| | Jan. | Feb. | Mar. | Apr. | May | Jun. | July | Aug. | Sep. | Oct. | Nov. | Dec. |
|---|---|---|---|---|---|---|---|---|---|---|---|---|
| Robin | | | | | | | | | | | | |
| Blackbird | | | | | | | | | | | | |
| Song thrush | | | | | | | | | | | | |
| Wren | | | | | | | | | | | | |
| Dunnock | | | | | | | | | | | | |

Bird song chart

Which bird species sings for the shortest time? Which bird
sings longest? Are there any bird species which sing in
every month of the year?

**Did you know?**

*Only the male cuckoo calls 'cuckoo' and he does it with his beak closed!*

# Song posts

Many birds have a favourite spot from which they sing. It may be the branch of a tree, a washing-line post, chimney pot, television aerial, telegraph pole or lamp post.

Make a sketch map of the song-posts of the birds in your garden, or in a small wood or park near your home. Do different birds prefer certain types of song-post?

What height song-post does each species prefer? There are several ways of estimating the height of tall objects. One of the simplest is to place a stick or piece of wood 1 metre long in front of the object you wish to measure. Stand some distance away and estimate how many times the stick goes into the height of the tree, lamp post or other object whose height you are trying to measure.

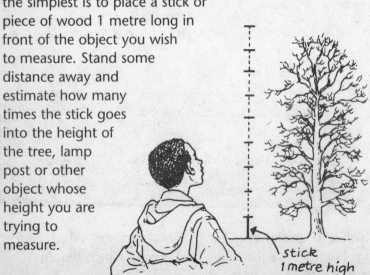

stick
1 metre high

# Recording bird song

To some extent, the recording of bird song is like bird photography: the more money you are able to spend on it, the more ambitious you can be. Nevertheless, quite satisfactory recordings can be made with a small portable tape recorder, if it has a separate microphone.

One of the biggest problems is wind noise, and a thin layer of foam rubber taped over the microphone will help to reduce this. Then tape the microphone to a stick and hold it in the vicinity of a singing bird.

foam rubber
taped over
microphone

microphone
tied to stick

## Birds on the move

Professional bird recordists use a large dish, called a parabolic reflector, to enable them to record sounds over a greater distance and to cut out unwanted sounds. You can make a parabolic reflector from an old dustbin lid or washing-up bowl. The microphone should be taped near the centre of the dustbin lid or bowl, although you will need to experiment to find the best position for it.

One of the most interesting experiments you can do is to play back the recorded sound of a bird to that bird! It will think that the song is being made by an intruder, and some aggressive birds, such as male robins, may actually attack the tape recorder. Most birds will then break into vigorous song, angry that another bird has dared to enter its territory.

By moving a tape recorder around a bird's territory, and playing its own song back to it, you can gradually discover where that bird's territory begins and ends. Avoid doing this too often, however, as it could distress birds, especially in the breeding season.

# Territories

When the time comes to breed, birds need an area around the nest which is undisturbed by other members of the same species. This is what we mean by a territory, and the territory may be very small, as for example in a nesting colony of gannets or guillemots, or very large, as in the case of a golden eagle. Birds will mark and defend their territory in various ways, including by singing and fighting off intruders.

You can map a bird's territory if you begin careful and patient observations in the early spring when many species are beginning to defend their territories quite vigorously. Robins are unusual in that they hold a territory, although not always the same one, throughout the year.

Begin by drawing a sketch-map of your own and neighbouring gardens or, if you don't have a garden, part of the local park, churchyard or recreation ground. Mark on it the spot where you regularly see a particular bird. Robins, blackbirds, song thrushes, great tits and chaffinches have a strong territorial instinct and it is a good idea to begin with one of these species. Mark on the map the song-posts of your chosen bird and the points where it drives off other birds of the same species. Note which birds your chosen individual gets worked up about, and which it ignores. Gradually you will build up a picture of your bird's territory.

## Did you know?

*Out of every 100 robins hatched in one year, only 28 are likely to survive until the following spring.*

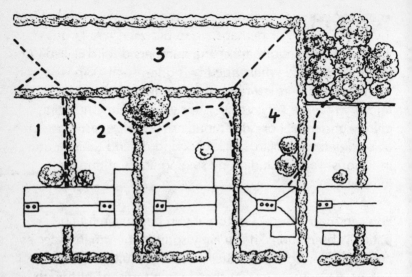

*Map of robins' territories*

# Road accident victims

It is estimated that every year more than 2.5 million birds are killed on Britain's roads, and an interesting, if somewhat sad, project is to survey these accident victims. You can do this on any stretch of busy road you travel along regularly, perhaps on your way to school each day. Always ask an adult to accompany you, stay on the pavement, and don't risk your own life doing this activity.

Every day record the number and species of birds that you find dead along your stretch of road and, if you have a map of the road, mark on it where each accident victim is found. Note whether the birds are young or adults.

In which month or months are most birds killed? Which species is the most frequent victim? Do young birds form a large proportion of the casualties during the summer months? Is there anything, such as a wall, hedge or tall tree by the roadside, or perhaps a gap between two large buildings, that might affect the numbers of birds killed? Are more birds killed when visibility is poor, such as in mist, fog or heavy rain? Are more birds killed during the early morning (count on your way to school), than are killed during the rest of the day (count again in the evening on your way home)?

### Did you know?

*Around the Mediterranean, over 100 million migrating birds are shot or trapped by hunters every year.*

# Bird strikes

Many birds are stunned, injured or even killed by flying into windows. There are several possible reasons for these accidents. The bird may be attracted by something in the room, or it may see its own reflection, which it then tries to attack. Or it may see the reflection of something outside in the garden, such as a bird table or a bird bath, which it tries to fly to. Another possibility is that crashes occur where there are windows at opposite ends of a room. If both windows are large, the bird may crash trying to fly straight through what it thinks is an open space.

You can increase our knowledge of these bird strikes if you keep records of them. Ask your friends, neighbours, and school mates, to tell you about any such accidents. Record the species involved and note whether or not the bird

recovered. Was the bird an adult or a juvenile? Describe
where the accident occurred and the weather conditions,
particularly the wind strength and direction, visibility, and
position of the sun. Suggest possible reasons for each strike.
What is the most common cause of these accidents to
birds?

# Preventing bird strikes

Most small birds keep well away from hawks, and you can
help to prevent birds flying into windows by making a
model hawk.

Make a large copy
of the hawk shape
on this page on
thin card. An old
cereal packet will
do. Carefully cut
around the edges
with scissors.

Colour the shape
black using a
crayon or paint.
Attach about 60
cm of string to the
head of the hawk
with sticky tape,

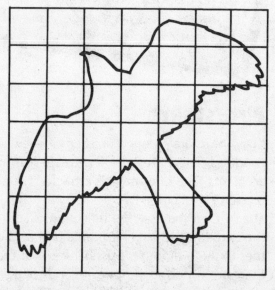

and use a drawing pin or sticky tape to fix it to the top of the
window frame.

Make hawk shapes for all the windows of your home which
birds have flown into. Make some more for your friends and
relatives to put up in their windows. By doing this, you will
be saving the lives of many birds.

# Birds in trouble

## Can you help?

Thousands of birds are injured or taken ill every year. In many cases there is nothing much you can do except find someone to put them out of their misery as soon as possible. Occasionally, though, you can do something to help.

## Orphans

Every year from April onwards, well-meaning people claim they have found 'orphaned' baby birds. Usually, however, these fledgelings have not been deserted at all but, having just left the nest, are being fed by their parents on the ground until they are able to fly.

*Fledgeling blackbird*

So if you do find a young bird that cannot fly, leave it where it is for its mother and father to find and feed. Only touch the baby bird if you need to move it somewhere safer, out of the reach of cats or cars.

## Birds in trouble

If you are absolutely certain that both parents are dead, put the baby bird in a cardboard box which is deep enough to prevent it from climbing out. Make a nest in the box out of several layers of cotton wool or crumpled newspaper, with a piece of soft cloth on top. Keep the box in a quiet, warm room while you call the RSPCA, PDSA or some other animal rescue society for help.

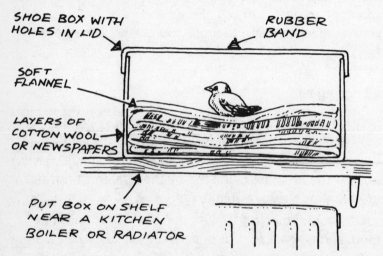

SHOE BOX WITH HOLES IN LID

RUBBER BAND

SOFT FLANNEL

LAYERS OF COTTON WOOL OR NEWSPAPERS

PUT BOX ON SHELF NEAR A KITCHEN BOILER OR RADIATOR

*How to look after an abandoned nestling or injured bird*

# Exhausted and starving birds

You usually come across exhausted or starving birds during very cold, snowy weather when natural supplies of food are almost impossible to find. Put the bird in a large, wire-fronted wooden box containing a perch. Keep it somewhere quiet and warm and give it food and water. In an emergency, any bird, large or small, will eat sultanas and brown bread soaked in water.

As soon as the weather has improved and the bird is fit and strong again, you can let it go.

# First aid

If you find a bird that has stunned itself by flying into a window, it will usually recover quickly if you can put it in a quiet dark place, such as a box with some small holes in the lid. Leave the bird there for a few hours until it becomes fully active again. Then you can release it. Similarly, keep an injured bird in a dark box while you call your local vet, or the RSPCA or PDSA for advice.

# Oiled sea birds

Increasing amounts of oil are spilt or deliberately dumped in the sea every year. The oil particularly affects those birds such as razorbills, puffins, guillemots and gannets which have to swim or dive through the oily surface of the sea to obtain their food.

The oil destroys the texture of the feathers so that the bird suffers from the cold and wet. The bird cannot hunt for food, and when it tries to preen itself, it may swallow some of the poisonous oil. An oiled bird is, therefore, likely to be in a very poor condition when it is eventually washed ashore.

If you find a bird covered with oil, don't try to clean it yourself. Take it to the nearest animal rescue society as quickly as possible. The local police station will usually be able to tell you where this is.

# 10 Making collections

## Pellets, feathers, footprints and nests

We are all collectors at heart and people collect everything from matchbox labels to antiques. There are a number of bird collections you can make that both look good and are informative although, of course, *it is illegal to collect birds' eggs, to take birds' nests while they are in use or to obtain feathers other than by picking up discarded ones.*

## Bird pellets

Birds of prey such as eagles, hawks and owls swallow small animals whole. They then get rid of the parts they cannot digest by coughing them up in a pellet. More than 60 British birds produce pellets, including rooks, crows, gulls, herons, robins and flycatchers. The pellets of owls are the easiest to start your collection with, as tawny owls are quite common, even in cities.

You can find owl pellets if you search beneath the bird's favourite roosting place, but make sure you are wearing your gloves when you collect them. Pellets don't smell and are not as nasty as you might think! Soak the pellets individually for several hours in jars of water to which you have added a few drops of disinfectant. Put the remains in a shallow dish and gently pull them apart, using tweezers and a large needle. Pick out the interesting bits. Look for the skulls of birds and mammals, fur and wing cases of beetles.

Mount the contents of one of the pellets on a piece of card. Say which bird made the pellet and where and when you collected it. Label the parts of the pellet if you can.

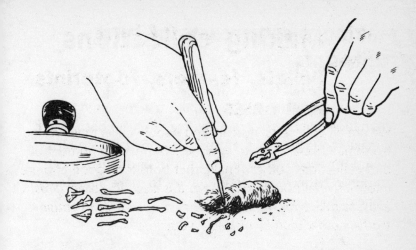

*Always wash your hands thoroughly after touching bird pellets.*

# Other food remains

You can also collect the food remains left by other birds. Whenever you see birds feeding on natural foods, wait quietly until they have left and then look for clues as to what they were eating. Make labelled collections of pine cones, hazelnuts, walnuts, acorns, cherry stones, snail shells and other foods that have been eaten by birds and also, if possible, by mammals such as squirrels, voles and mice.

Such a collection will be very useful if you later find food remains but have not seen the bird or other animal responsible for leaving them.

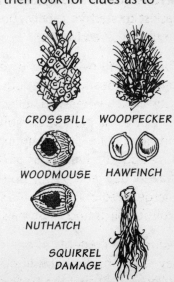

CROSSBILL  WOODPECKER

WOODMOUSE  HAWFINCH

NUTHATCH

SQUIRREL
DAMAGE

# Making plaster casts of bird footprints

When you are out birdwatching, you may come across a clear footprint made by a bird walking across mud. Alternatively, you could rake an area of soil smooth, wet it to make it muddy and then sprinkle some breadcrumbs around the muddy area and wait for a bird to leave its footprints. Either way, you might like to make a plaster cast of one of the footprints.

 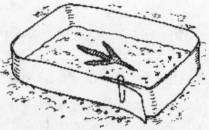

Choose a complete footprint and, using tweezers, carefully pick out any leaves or twigs.

Surround the footprint with a strip of thin card. Push the card well into the mud without disturbing the print.

Put a little water into an old basin or large clean margarine tub. Use a dry spoon to add some plaster of Paris powder to the water. Stir the mixture with a clean stick. Add more plaster of Paris powder until the mixture feels like thick cream.

Gently pour the liquid plaster into the circle. Tap the sides carefully to get rid of any air bubbles. Add more plaster of Paris if necessary.

Leave the plaster for 30 minutes to an hour to set. Then carefully dig it up and take it home.

The next day, brush off any mud and peel off the card. Wash the cast in cold water. Paint the footprint with poster paint and label it with the name of the bird which made the footprint.

N.B. Only by trial and error will you get the plaster mixture just right. So why not practise by getting a pet dog or cat to walk in a tray of wet mud for you?

# Collecting feathers

Collect clean feathers from gardens, parks, woods and fields. Look at them with a hand lens to see how they are made up. The flat part of the feather is called the vane. Run it between your fingers and you will see it is formed of minute hooked branches which fit neatly together.

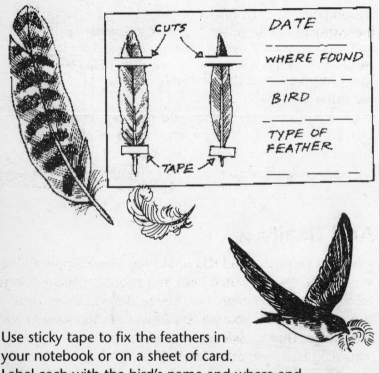

Use sticky tape to fix the feathers in your notebook or on a sheet of card. Label each with the bird's name and where and when you found it. You could also collect the feathers scattered from week to week where flocks of birds gather. Mount each week's collection on a card and, by comparing several cards, you will be able to discover the order in which birds moult different types of feathers.

# Collecting birds' nests

Most birds build new nests each year, so you can sometimes collect old nests in the autumn when the birds have finished with them – providing no other bird or animal is using them!

If you do find an empty nest, collect it in dry weather, wearing gloves. Then follow the instructions on pp. 90–1 for de-lousing the nest.

Don't forget to label the nest with the name of the kind of bird that made it and where and when you found it. If you want, you could mount it on a stand like the one shown in the picture here.

# And finally...

Now that you have read this book, you should know a little more about how to watch birds and about the many things you can do to help them. Feel free to develop these ideas and experiment for yourself. Do all you can to expand your knowledge. That knowledge will help to preserve the remaining birds and other forms of wildlife that share our planet.

Birdwatching in any form is a fun, inexpensive hobby. It will repay you over and over again in terms of excitement, good health and the sharpening of your eye, ear and brain. It has endless possibilities, so – good luck and good sleuthing!

# Taking it further
## Organisations and books

### Useful organisations

If you are a young ornithologist working alone at home, you may want to meet other young people with the same kind of interests or to seek help from older, more expert birdwatchers. There is no point in discovering new and exciting things about birds if you are not able to share that information with other interested people. Why not join one of the clubs listed below?

### Young Ornithologists' Club (YOC)
The Lodge, Sandy, Bedfordshire SG19 2DL
This is the junior section of the RSPB (see below) and is the world's biggest wildlife club for young people. Members receive a magazine six times a year (to which you can send your discoveries), free entry to over 100 bird reserves and information on activities, events, holidays and competitions.

### Royal Society for the Protection of Birds (RSPB)
The Lodge, Sandy, Bedfordshire SG19 2DL
The RSPB runs many nature reserves in Great Britain and campaigns nationally for the interests of birds.

### RSPCA
Junior Membership, The Causeway, Horsham,
West Sussex RH12 1HG

### Wildlife Watch
The Green, Witham Park, Waterside South, Lincoln LN5 7JR
The junior branch of The Wildlife Trusts. Local Wildlife Watch Groups run meetings all over the country.

## Wildfowl and Wetlands Trust
Slimbridge, Gloucester GL2 7BT
Mainly concerned with the conservation and study of ducks, geese and swans and marshes and other wetlands.

## The British Trust for Ornithology
The Nunnery, Thetford, Norfolk IP24 2PU

Another useful organisation for you to get in touch with is your local County Wildlife Trust. There are 47 of these trusts in Great Britain and between them they manage over 2,200 nature reserves. Contact them if you want to know about wildlife and nature reserves and activities in your area. Ask your local library for their address, or write to

## The Wildlife Trusts
The Green, Witham Park, Waterside South, Lincoln LN5 7JR

Your local bird recorder is based at the County Bird Club, details of which are available at your local library.

# Useful books and recordings

*Collins New Generation Guide to Birds of Britain and Europe*
by Christopher Perrins
(HarperCollins)

*Wings Guide to British Birds*
by Dominic Couzens
(HarperCollins)

*Birdwatcher's Pocket Book*
by Peter Hayman
(Mitchell Beazley)

*Easy Bird Guide*
by Peter Hayman and Rob Hume
(Macmillan)

## Taking it further

*Birdfeeder Handbook*
by Robert Burton
(Dorling Kindersley)

*Eyewitness Guides: Bird*
by David Burnie
(Dorling Kindersley)

*Collins Field Guide: Bird Songs and Calls of Britain and Northern Europe*
by Geoff Sample
(HarperCollins)
(contains two CDs and a book to help you identify bird sounds)

*Birds: A Guide Book to British Birds*
by Jonathan Elphick
(BBC Worldwide) and
*Birds: A Video Guide to British Birds*
by Tony Soper
(BBC Worldwide)
(available separately or together in one pack)

# Websites

A brilliant way to pass on and receive information about birds is via the Internet. There are literally hundreds of bird and birding websites now and this is just a selection.

### LINKS TO LOTS OF OTHER BIRD SITES
**Birdbase:** http://home.sol.no/~tibjonn/index.htm
**Birdlinks:** http://www.phys.rug.nl/mk/people/wpv/birdlink.html
**Birdlinks:**
    http://wwwis.cs.utwente.nl:8080/deby/Birds/birdlink.html
**Bird Links to the World:**
    http://www.ntic.qc.ca/~nellus/links2.html
(NB These last three are all different despite the similar names.)

## UK/EUROPE
**Birdguides:** http://www.birdguides.com/index.html
**Bird on:** http://birdcare.com/birdon/
**Birdwatch Magazine:** http://www.birdwatch.co.uk
**Eurobirdnet:** http://ebn.unige.ch/ebn
**interBirdNet:**
    http://dspace.dial.pipex.com/town/square/gf09/index.html
**Irish Birdwatching:**
    http://www.geocities.com/RainForest/2801/index.html
**UK 400 Club:** http://www.uk400.demon.co.uk/

## BIRD SOUNDS
**Birdsounds:** http://www.valmet.com/kyyroju/birdsounds.htm

## BIRD PICTURES
**RSPB Images:**
    http://www.rspb-images.co.uk/html/homepage.htm
**VIREO:** http://www.acnatsci.org/vireo

## AMERICAN
**American Birding Association:**
    http://www.americanbirding.org
**Birding on the Web:** http://www.birder.com/
**National Audubon:**
    http://www.audubon.org/audubon/contents.html
**Ornithological Information Source:**
    http://www.nmnh.si.edu/BIRDNET/
**Peterson Online:** http://www.petersononline.com/
**Thayer Birding Software:**
    http://www.birding.com/default.asp

## OTHER
**African Bird Club:**
    http://www.netlink.co.uk/users/aw/abchome.html
**Neotropical Bird Club:**
    http://www.netlink.co.uk/users/aw/nbchome.html
**Oriental Bird Club:**
    http://www.netlink.co.uk/users/aw/obchome.html
**OSME:** http://www.netlink.co.uk/users/ag/osme/osmehome.

# Glossary

**bill** Another name for beak.

**bird of prey** A bird that lives by killing and eating other animals.

**breeding season** The time of year, usually spring, when birds find a mate, build a nest and rear young.

**camouflage** Colours and patterns that blend with a bird's background and hide it from enemies.

**colony** A group of birds of the same species nesting close together.

**dabbling** A way of feeding in lakes or ponds where birds run their beaks along the surface of the water while straining food from it.

**extinct** Not existing any more.

**fledgling** A young bird that has just started to fly.

**flock** A large group of birds moving around together.

**glide** To fly with wings kept still and stretched out.

**habitat** The natural home of a bird, animal or plant.

**instinct** A form of behaviour that some animals are born with. It does not have to be learnt.

**migration** Long-distance journeys made by some birds, according to the seasons, usually between their nesting area and wintering area.

**moulting** The shedding of feathers, usually once or twice a year. In most birds, feathers drop out singly as new ones grow underneath.

**nestling** A bird too young to leave the nest.

**pellet** The undigested part of a bird's food which it ejects through its beak.

**plumage** A bird's covering of feathers.

**predator** A bird or other animal that hunts and kills birds or other animals for food.

**prey** Animals that are hunted and eaten as food by predators.

**roost** To sleep. (The place where birds roost is also called a roost.)

**soar** To rise or fly high in the air.

**species** Any one kind of animal (including a bird) or plant. Members of a species are all very similar and adult males and females can breed with each other and produce young.

**territory** An area of land in which a bird or animal lives, feeds and breeds. Other birds or animals entering the territory are attacked, particularly in the breeding season.

# Index

# Index

# ACTIVATORS

## All you need to know

| | | | |
|---|---|---|---|
| 0 340 715162 | Astronomy | £3.99 | ☐ |
| 0 340 715197 | Ballet | £3.99 | ☐ |
| 0 340 715847 | Birdwatching | £3.99 | ☐ |
| 0 340 715189 | Cartooning (Sept 98) | £3.99 | ☐ |
| 0 340 715200 | Computers Unlimited (Sept 98) | £3.99 | ☐ |
| 0 340 715111 | Cycling | £3.99 | ☐ |
| 0 340 715219 | Drawing (Sept 98) | £3.99 | ☐ |
| 0 340 715138 | Football | £3.99 | ☐ |
| 0 340 715146 | The Internet | £3.99 | ☐ |
| 0 340 715170 | Riding | £3.99 | ☐ |
| 0 340 715235 | Skateboarding | £3.99 | ☐ |
| 0 340 71512X | Swimming (Sept 98) | £3.99 | ☐ |

Turn the page to find out how to order these books

## more info • more tips • more fun!

# ORDER FORM

Books in the Activators series are available at your local bookshop, or can be ordered direct from the publisher. A complete list of titles is given on the previous page. Just tick the titles you would like and complete the details below. Prices and availability are subject to change without prior notice.

Please enclose a cheque or postal order made payable to Bookpoint Ltd, and send to: Hodder Children's Books, Cash Sales Dept, Bookpoint, 39 Milton Park, Abingdon, Oxon OX14 4TD. Email address: orders@bookpoint.co.uk.

If you would prefer to pay by credit card, our call centre team would be delighted to take your order by telephone. Our direct line is 01235 400414 (lines open 9.00 am – 6.00 pm, Monday to Saturday; 24-hour message answering service). Alternatively you can send a fax on 01235 400454.

Title ......... First name ....................... Surname ...................................

Address ...................................................................................................

................................................................................................................

................................................................................................................

Daytime tel ..................................... Postcode...................................

If you would prefer to post a credit card order, please complete the following.

Please debit my Visa/Access/Diner's Card/American Express (delete as applicable) card number:

| | | | | | | | | | | | | | | | | | | |
|--|--|--|--|--|--|--|--|--|--|--|--|--|--|--|--|--|--|--|--|

Signature .......................................................Expiry Date ...................

If you would NOT like to receive further information on our products, please tick ☐.